AT
FIRST
&
THEN

AT FIRST & THEN

POEMS

Danielle Rose

www.blacklawrence.com

Executive Editor: Diane Goettel
Chapbook Editor: Kit Frick
Book and Cover Design: Amy Freels
Cover Art: "Isadora Duncan in the Parthenon, Athens." Photograph by Edward Jean Steichen / Wikimedia Commons

Published 2021 by Black Lawrence Press.
Printed in the United States.

Contents

at first

"It is in large part according to the sounds people make that we judge them sane or insane, male or female, good, evil, trustworthy, depressive, marriageable, moribund, likely or unlikely to make war on us, little better than animals, inspired by God."
—Anne Carson, "The Gender of Sound"

ekphrasis on
"the most beautiful suicide"

because especially in death
a woman's body is not her own
if she had been paint
then the limousine an improvised canvas
and the gawking crowds
guests at some bizarre performance
instead it is crossed ankles arms arcing inward
as if warding against an attempt to steal her secrets
like me she wanted to disappear
i have too many of my mother's tendencies
perhaps she nervously tapped her foot
was no fun at parties and did not understand
that she was not actually broken
how i invent her a fiction from the tangles
of such real things
a spectacular line from a magazine
seven short sentences
where she expressed her need to be nothing
and we ignored her wishes
maybe this is why i am so easily seduced by violence
by how it fills the empty spaces with something i desire
that is not quite love
when they tried to move her she spilled
how a human being can become
water! slipping through our hands

aleister crowley summoned demons & all i get is this tarot telling me i am always in the wrong

i want to become a fountain / first still stone / then bubbling water
like seeping / like an underground stream that swells beneath
us / but i still lacquer myself in protections like how a graveyard
becomes an ocean
        / like how i launder
my filth & then keep scrubbing / what is a stain but something we
keep washing / because i want to become my mother's high cabinet
/ where she kept her gods behind plastic containers / i just want to
stop asking questions about how i began / & flow like a fountain / i
can be still stone / i can be the water / always gently rippling / i want
to write this poem like a means to become corrected again & again
becoming / another round of scrubbing

variations on the death of tinkerbell

keeling over this is meant to appear as suddenness
    like cardiac arrest or seizure / but there is no emergency team
        only a solitary clapping or how we understand pride

as the condition to possess a life / she hides behind a leaf
    like i pull on a blanket of adjectives or close
        doors in the face of my shame / it is almost like playing house

or playing at life / where keeling over is meant
    to be a call for help she can't help herself
        but to wither without a spotlight

& i am so like her except i cannot close the door / cannot shut
    anything out / she is more like a lima bean
        curled on the floor than a creature of light

so the viewer is reminded that she is a small thing / surrounded
    by such bigness so unlike her bigness / this is a murder /
        like flickering lamps a simple metaphor for death

this is because when light keels over it is a call / a call for help
    but she cannot help herself so we clap and scream
        like she was actually dying / and not just

a flicker of the light / keeling over / this is a murder / this is bloody
    & her light is leaking / clap / scream / & i don't understand
        i'm just a kid clapping because i don't want

the human body contains enough bones to construct a complete skeleton

& it is a lie to say that women have one additional rib / that they were raised from the earth / sculpted in a garden like how we hang tomatoes / remember how seeds are little moments of the possible / like asking what we desire of the things that grow inside of us / maybe a fireplace filled with the family songs that were forgotten / a line of rilke about bridges just off the tongue / & i talk about what i might contain / i spin seeds & spit something out / if i were an electrical socket i might call myself lucent / but there are over 200 bones inside of me & i cannot feel them unless they are broken / i could build a bridge from what i contain / just off the tongue a way to cross a dangerous crevasse / to sing songs & sew seeds / i want us to raise from the earth / become a question for mathematics like counting bones inside of a moving body / spinning like a sequin & then coming to rest / complete / i dream that adam was a liar & just wanted to feel less alone

on the creation of new language from the reading lists of the dead

after a death / when i taste my own need like unpleasant iron bleeding behind a bad tooth / this is when i become like blankets in winter / it is how loss reveals a new language / & why at night i wonder why the sound of a faucet running brings panic / or why the sight of an owl in flight makes my heart race with joy / there is small magic in how suddenly my kitchen feels like a different home / & where the rough edge of that chipped dinner plate becomes a flowerbed & then blooms / there are even discarded bits of paper raining like poems / raining like so many useless poems / because grandmother you read *ulysses* when you were sixteen but you will never read my poems / so i can only believe that soil is just one way to cover a grave / & that burial is ever-present

in the graveyard / three men in yellow reflective vests / heap dirt into an open wound

on forgery

when i hear sirens i become a tightened coil—this is a way to explain
that i am something that is ready—but i cannot smell by flicking a
cautious tongue—i must leap like a gazelle or slide my hands over my
hips—this body is a serpent—it is a thing that becomes ready & then
molts—& i am not ready—i was coursing venom & searching
desperately for another word to call myself drowned—this is a body
that fights me—because i didn't fight back i didn't even know i was
fighting—i just kept pounding my fists & never learned how to not
lie—this body is a lie i hear sirens & it is always back to that moment—
handcuffed—anguine stumbling drunk barely able to stand—stuffed
into an ambulance—the neighborhood became a pit of copperheads
& i vanished

in which i explain to socrates why i am bottling my secrets into a jar

it is how i can beg permission / to be the way sunrise is both the bedroom window & a way to open it wide / because this is difficult work / like climbing a mountain or falling out of love / & in my dreams i am a chunk of marble to be carved / but this is not a doorway that likes to open / i am meddling in dangerous things / this is a search for coalescence between heartbeats / & how to live with the things that make such demands of me / like choosing the color of my candor / or how ants carry their fallen / if i were a geyser i would just be quiet / bubbling at a murmur / but this is a rushing river & the rapids overtake me / with all this begging i have trouble breathing / i have trouble being a dollhouse when all the tiny furniture is broken / if my pleading were an anchor i could moor a ship / but i am akin to flotsam / perhaps i could be a sunken treasure & a forgotten maritime grave / when i write these poems i want them to circumvent this memory / to keep my secrets while also telling them / so when diotima claims all acts of creation are poetry i just agree & remain quiet

tell me i'm prettier when i smile

because i do not desire to be a road pocked with potholes / but these scowls gouge the path ahead like too many pecking crows / & this is entirely a dream i can wake from if i can just find the right phrase / like *i am a kiln & i become a burnt orange* / the sounds stretch & yet i am still dreaming / & this stretching does not decide for me it is a lesson in constraint / like how i want to build rhetorical arguments from children's balloons / i want to watch them soar & disappear & become just another dot of clear sky / tell me i am like the sky / & lie to me / tell me i am expansive & clear / i need to hear that joyful clouds reach their hands into my chest / because i can feel them inside of me / storming / telling me i am pretty when i smile / i want to be a set of cascading conditions / like a logical proof or the way i am always sneaking away from my fear / tell me i am prettier when i smile / tell me / become a cloud & tell me that when i am pretty / it is impossible to be so empty

on walking outside with my morning coffee at 9:00 am to find my new neighbors fucking like cottontails in their backyard

at first innocent like sunbathing
just so much skin
& two bodies glimpsed between branches
like some low-rent adam & eve
frolicking
rocking their hips like a ship in rough seas
                                    & i couldn't look away
as they became two horseflies learning to swim
all their crooked legs dangling
& if i could catch them
i would place them in a jar
to watch them fuck
against a snapped twig
on a clot of moss to make them feel
more at home in their prison
                           am i jealous? perhaps
if i could stretch myself
& become a way to rock my hips like a propeller
but when i see them fucking
i am the vastness of an ocean teeming
with undiscovered life
                          this thrusting & rocking
is spellcraft
is a gesture
is a certain sound
& then something happens
like the smell of water or how we tuck ourselves

into such small spaces
because in the next yard over they're fucking
& i'm thinking about ways to become a rainstorm
how if the sky just opened up
something would grow
& their panting would bloom

if i believed in the ninth step i might

want / & then count the number of bottles like rings in a tree to
determine age / because to make restitution is economic here
someone has to give / & another must take so we might make
commerce / or sacrifice / measured by how many apologies I can
fit in my mouth / & you aren't even there / because this is all fuck-
off hypothetical like screaming at god or understanding the self
/ which are both ways to avoid the question of justice / if these
arms were lengthy enough they could stretch all the way to our
beginnings / like an ancient tree or a thirteen-year-old boy falling
from it / who used to be me / just as drunkenness was once me / how
disappointment was once me / & how i was every hurtful noise / how
do we grow to be able to touch where everything started / to give
restitution without worry or fear / because i am terrified of looking
into a shattered mirror / & seeing monsters wearing my old face

gender swap potion

ingredients
1 cup of odd childhood dreams
½ cup vegetable oil
2 tablespoons of my mother's tears
4 cloves of unresolved trauma, minced
2 oz of pervasive discomfort
1 teaspoon of coarse cracked black pepper
1½ teaspoons bitter salt
1 large root of all this disquiet, cut into small 1" cubes
2 decades of desperation
a pinch of sugar
1 boy, in pieces

directions
1. stir together liquid & emotional ingredients in a large mixing
bowl until they are well-blended.
2. crack each decade like an egg allowing the bitterness & hurt to
drip like yolk into the terrified bowl. beat mercilessly. add a pinch
of sugar to taste.
3. gently stir in the unresolved trauma, bitter salts & black pepper.
4. heat to a boil & then just constantly reduce & reduce & reduce
until you cannot believe you can become any smaller & still be able
to speak. remove from heat.
5. add cubed disquiet to reduction & stir until softened, 2-3
minutes.
6. pour over pieces of boy & allow 2 years to marinate.

& then

"I have not and never did have any motive of poetry
But to achieve clarity."
—George Oppen, "Route"

this is a trans poem about swans

which begins in the boston garden / where people sit inside giant wooden swans

& i am the swan / this is normal / i watch the families cross the footbridge like balloons let adrift or pigeons darting after scraps of bread / because this is a long journey / it is something like orpheus a vertical transformation / but i could not pretend to cultivate myself like a garden / this body is something i am forced to touch when i suddenly grasp for love in the middle of the night / i want to become a myth that travels under & then above again but emerges different / to become something beautiful like a swan fleeing from itself forever / this is a trans poem about swans & i desperately wish for it to be beautiful / but beauty does not escape & become a silent parking lot / in an emergency it cannot be trusted to shuffle quickly toward the nearest exit / it will never bring me away from where this body started / & so i am the swan / opened / because this is a trans poem about swans we must see entrails spilling / her flesh cut open with surgical precision / this is my body a temple under renovation / a pristine bright surgical center / a way to perhaps swim forward / after

variations on drawing down the moon

it is about drawing things in. i want
to be tree roots / & lightning
striking an open field.

how first i open myself like the face
of the moon / so that i become
the face of the moon.

& into me flows the face of the moon.
goddess / descend into me
through me into the earth.

it is about remaining open like how
     i want to be tree roots / to hold
     you both hopeful & ashamed

that i may be unfaithful / i imagine
     that i am tree leaves & they
     drink in the moonlight

& into me flows the hungry moon.
goddess / projection / demon
whatever just enter me now.

this is how you drink
divinity / & perhaps why
tides swell. in both there is dancing.

arms toward the sky / you drink god
then she seeps out again.
this must be how

we can bear to be so empty / so
we can be so full / so we can be tree root
drawing ourselves into the moon.

body maps

body map #1
where the cartographer is confused they approximate   markings
of depth & elevation become smudged ink   this is the science of
border disputes & mass transit   because *all models are wrong*   because
the map is a violence   because the face is a map   because my face
is the map   because my face has changed & no longer accurately
represents the map

body map #2
to think there were so many shoeboxes filled with old photographs
printed on old photo paper   & none of them were me   what a
strangeness to not recognize oneself   like how i cannot write
poems about missing children   or why i won't go swimming
these are the things we choose to avoid   the tracing of bodies to
mark latitudes & longitudes   endless hours of comparison   what
it means to become *exposed*   because we do not pretend to hold the
same map nor do our travels meet   still you chart my body for me

body map #3
because i will insist upon the importance of violence   the scrapes
& cuts caused by placing the map of desire upon this territory of my
body   to mold to the elevation lines & cool blue oceans   i can feel
the swell of sea & shift of mountains under my skin   to be measured
is what it means to be temporary   & everything before this did not
work

the word "embrace" was born of holding things upright like a pillar or this idea

that virginity / is to not know what to do with this body its holes its
implements used to grasp / & i am a newness

like birth but nestled within an after / like how seeds spread &
they will become more seeds / grow more stamen because plants
understand how to fuck / they wait for the sun to be just right / &
then they bloom alone i am coal / wire / chicken feed scattered on
a barnyard floor / hands grasp & i am consumed pecking / the way
smoke moves through light both intangible & ultimately abiding /
ceasing this body its plugs & sockets / & i know this is filling / this
isn't taking / this is bracing me against a body & then not falling

when my therapist asks me to briefly describe my experience of childhood

metaphorically an egg would be too easy & it was a meat-sack not a hard encasement like a hospital room not pulling the covers over your head when you're afraid in the dark

if i could avoid the question i might begin to run and try to become a tepid mountaintop that cannot maintain snow like how to avoid saying *i blossomed* or *she was always inside of me*

this is a task made immeasurably more difficult by its adjacency to my transness as all things adjacent to my transness are made more difficult

i am a queer body that was hidden inside a different queer body

sometimes i wish that i was a sculpture carved from the cadence of rainfall & then by the absence of rainfall

i want to be for once sitting so still like lakewater at dawn but i am six families of four frolicking on the beach rubbing sunscreen laughing splashing in the shallow disturbed water not discussing how they all hate each other

maybe a beach ball inside of another beach ball but the one on the outside was never quite right

body as the disrupted migratory habits of new england mourning doves

Each year the doves fly south. Like the body, they are endless in their migration *toward* & *away*. The process is not "easy" as humans would say. Birds do not understand "easy." In fact, we do not know if the birds even have a word for *ease*. Instead, their movements are the calibrated result of *need*. Doves must breed, safely nest & eat; doves are concerned, foremost, with their own survival. The body encounters a phenomena of sameness, it requires comfort & safety & sustenance. While the doves embark upon long journeys toward ideas that become memory these bodies become memory.

Consider first the act of preparation: A migrating dove must travel hundreds of miles in search of winter feeding grounds. This is a process of exchange. The bird exchanges body mass for energy in flight. This is mathematical. A mourning dove will carefully alter their metabolism to survive & thrive during the rigors of flight. It is argued that this is genetic. Birds do what birds do. They will feed & rest & preen & molt. This is migration when it occurs *toward* or *away*.

Once prepared for their journey, doves will fly south in smaller pieces that slowly become more whole. It begins with a distinct avian restlessness when the young take notice of the shortening days & new winds carried by creeping Autumn. Soon after the females will flee the frayed ends of their summer nests followed still some time after by the males. Be reminded that doves do not understand our human things they simply desire to not die.

The doves do not know that the human body is comprised of eleven elements, or that our thoughts are literally electric. Like birds we eat & drink & conserve our energies. Like birds we migrate along our own latitudinal lines, moving up & down rungs on our unsturdy ladders. A dove will prepare extensively for their journey; human beings are most frequently taken abruptly by what an ornithologist would certainly call *disruption*.

Disruption is when something *happens* that was unexpected & a populous is scattered or broken. Among doves, common causes could include a sudden increase in predator activity or an unsubstantiated population boon.

Disruption is unexpected like a flat tire or someone lingering their eyes too long in the subway. Humans do not travel flyways down the coast nor do they forage in dirt for small insects & worms. Remember this while you consider that bodies are constantly in disruption always pushing against each other to get more space. Mourning doves fly 1,500 miles to winter feeding grounds in flocks of chirping birds singing calls—they don't sit alone in the middle of the night running their fingers against the bones of their ribcage. Doves take off & fill the sky & then they get to leave somewhere *away* but this body is here like it is always here. When the doves are disrupted they leave but where do we get to go?

if the body is a prison-house where is the warden i have some complaints about the plumbing

> "The idea that the body is a prison-house, to which the soul is condemned for past misdeeds, is attributed by Plato to the Orphics."
> —*The Republic*, trans. Cornford

they ask / if this is my body // & i ~~lie~~ say yes

it might start with the conspicuous absence of childhood photos—then a process of testing for misidentification—questions that begin with oh please suddenly a hot iron scratching my stomach—& so i am learning to call unpleasant histories by their real names—such as what i demand of love—& that i used to be a boy—to think that if this body was a prison what happened when i escaped—i know that poetry is not light—& that we do not need another word for empty—i still do not know how to say that he put his hands all over me—or that i wanted to like it even though i did not—to think a dove will fly 1,500 miles to fuck & sometimes i can't even leave the couch—even plato does not want to admit responsibility so he blames someone else too

how to write a poem while attending my first aa meeting in over a year

firmly grasp that the truth is fragile
for instance one could give any name
or not even be an addict
i will believe them & that is beautiful
remember each meeting is a variation
voices desperate to lose themselves in each other
same book same collection plate
all the different ways they weigh sin
& how i don't care that regulars
make plans for coffee discuss healthcare
or that i never really chose a higher power
i am counting the exits from this basement
while the man sitting beside me asks
& are you married? i just smile
because i cannot stomach to break the truth
the way i used to break the truth
so maybe our names aren't real
in the same way that my heart will sometimes stop
perhaps this is what i mean
when i say that a poem is always there
my worry waiting to fold these little moments
of sadness into something else
desperate & untrue

when i touch myself i think about a hand rubbing circles on my back

because want is like a hammer / & i flatten
like a paper fan / here is an analogy
it is grasslands then a forest
& then grasslands again

i am thinking
about a hand on my back
rubbing circles / & i flutter

like a girl discussing all the possibility
in the words *one day maybe* / & if this is where my mind
travels during sex i cannot be a temple / i will not
become a cloud of incense & just quietly depart

because between my legs
is a valley i named & renamed & dedicated
again & again / on my back a hand a birdsong
a sudden frost / a detour / a way to make myself
into a fondness that calmly drowns

pretty in soft light

like how eyebrows are a lie / & how this is plucking something out or
taking a razor to rawness again & again / i concern myself first with
methods to interrogate birdsong / & then with scouring this old
thesaurus for a word that means / *this body is a cascading series of discomforts*
                       & desperate for things it does not
understand / like men & women falling in love / i only imagine
romance like licking lips and too-long stares on the subway / never
these clever methods to devour a persistent yearning / i just want a
machine that turns a raincloud into dreams / i want to look in the
mirror & decide that *yes i am pretty in soft light* / pretty like a swarm of bees
passed out drunk
                in a yellow flowerbed / pollen
                floating / all in soft light so pretty

an inventory of things that have changed

mirrors   gravity   the smell of flowers   men staring
fear of insects   doors ahead   the color of desire
how i spell my name   my name   the length of daylight
stories   like how   i became   daylily   a mountain
a length   of verse   piercing   my tongue   this joy
our love   understanding   my joy   these mirrors   sex
how i know love   & just
        joy   joy   joy   joy

acknowledgments

I am grateful to the editors of the publications that previously featured work contained in this volume.

"ekphrasis on 'the most beautiful suicide'" first appeared in *The Shallow Ends*

"aleister crowley summoned demons & all i get is this tarot telling me i am always in the wrong" & "in which i explain to socrates why i am bottling my secrets into a jar" first appeared in *Empty Mirror*

"variations on the death of tinkerbell" first appeared in *Random Sample Review*

"on the creation of new language from the reading lists of the dead" first appeared in *Kissing Dynamite*

"tell me i'm prettier when i smile" first appeared in *Okay Donkey*

"if i believed in the ninth step i might" first appeared in *Barren Magazine*

"gender swap potion" first appeared in *Moonchild Magazine*

"this is a trans poem about swans" first appeared in *Pidgeonholes*

"variations on drawing down the moon" first appeared in *Luna Luna*

"body maps" first appeared in *Random Sample Review*

"the word 'embrace' was born of holding things upright like a pillar or this idea" first appeared in *YES Poetry*

"body as the disrupted migratory habits of new england mourning doves" first appeared in *Dovecote Magazine*

"if the body is a prison-house where is the warden i have some complaints about the plumbing" first appeared in *Third Point Press*

"when i touch myself i think about a hand rubbing circles on my back" first appeared in *Q/A Poetry*

"pretty in soft light" first appeared in *Glass Poetry*

Photo: Lola Arellano-Fryer

Danielle Rose is a poet and prose-writer from Massachusetts. Her work can be found in publications such as *Palette Poetry, Sundog Lit,* & *The Shallow Ends. at first & then* is her first chapbook.